CARIBOO MAGI

Lucia Frangione

Talonbooks

Vancouver

Copyright © 2005 Lucia Frangione

Talonbooks
P.O. Box 2076, Vancouver, British Columbia, Canada V6B 3S3
www.talonbooks.com

Typeset in Bembo and printed and bound in Canada.

First Printing: 2005

The publisher gratefully acknowledges the financial support of the Canada
Council for the Arts; the Government of Canada through the Book
Publishing Industry Development Program; and the Province of British
Columbia through the British Columbia Arts Council for our publishing
activities.

Library and Archives Canada Cataloguing in Publication

Frangione, Lucia
       Cariboo magi / Lucia Frangione.

A play.
ISBN 0-88922-527-3

       I. Title.

PS8561.R27755C37 2005   C812'.54   C2005-902471-2

Cariboo Magi was originally commissioned by Lambs Players in San Diego, California, as a one-act play; it was produced in November 2000 and directed by Jeff Miller. The full-length version was first produced by Pacific Theatre in Vancouver, British Columbia, on November 30, 2001 with the following cast and crew:

JOE MACKEY . . . . John James Hong*
MADAME FANNY DUBEAU . . . . Lucia Frangione*
REVEREND WILLIAM TELLER . . . . . . Dirk Van Stralen
MARTA REDDY . . . . Donna-lea Ford*

Director: Diane Brown*
Stage manager: Allen Thompson
Dramaturge: Lisa C. Ravensbergen
Historical Research: Don Noble
Set and lighting design: Kevin McAllister
Costumes: Rebekka Sorensen

The play runs for one hour and fifty-five minutes with one intermission.

Though based around historical events, the characters in this play and their actions are purely fictional. Any relation to real life events or people is unintentional.

---

* Artists appeared courtesy of the Canadian Actors Equity Association

The play opens on the Cariboo Wagon Road, British Columbia, in November 1870, then sails ahead to Fanny Dubeau's saloon in San Diego. In the second act, our troupe ends up making their way north on a steamer, then up the Cariboo Wagon Road to the gold rush town of Barkerville, BC, arriving on Christmas Eve.

DRAMATIS PERSONAE

JOE MACKEY

Mackey is a young, self-proclaimed confederate poet in his early twenties and has more enthusiasm than he does talent. He came to the Cariboo as an Overlander in 1865 from Ontario to make his fortune in gold, but by the time he got there, all the good claims were gone. He ended up working as a translator for the mines because of his great proficiency in languages. Mackey's an orphan of mixed lineage, likely Chinese and British; he simply calls himself a Canadian when asked. He's ready to find himself a wife.

MADAME FANNY DUBEAU

Fanny is allegedly from Paris, France; she was mysteriously widowed in San Francisco and started her own reputable saloon in Old Town, San Diego, with "terpsichorean artiste" dancing girls and a small repertory theatre company. Since Horton opened his hotel in New Town, her business has suffered greatly and she's being forced to close it down. Her elegant veneer thinly hides a cunning, avaricious businesswoman. She's been twenty-six for at least five years.

REVEREND WILLIAM TELLER

A defunct Anglican minister. He initially came from England to plant churches and save the souls of gold miners. He held his first services in the San Francisco saloons then moved to San Diego to see if he could save the soul of whalers, which proved even more difficult. All his hard work and fervour over the years seemed to have been in vain and he finally succumbed to drink and despair. He is a well-educated, hopelessly romantic and articulate man who frequents Fanny's saloon so often that he knows all the words to the plays. He's probably in his early thirties but he feels like he's in his late sixties.

MARTA REDDY

Marta was a ten-year-old German girl when she was sold to a boss hurdy, dragged to the New World in the hull of a boat and subsequently bought by Fanny, who trained her as an actor and singer and transformed her into a child star. Fanny made a lot of money by keeping Marta adolescent far beyond her years. She bound her breasts, stuck her in kinder dirndl and had her play Gertrude in *The Little Treasure* for a weekly pittance, room and board. Eventually, Marta demanded to be treated like a full-grown woman so she could mature into leading roles, but Fanny wouldn't allow it. Marta is now twenty-two, blunt, childish, naïve and hot-tempered.

AMERICAN POST, CREDITOR, MR. BOWRON

These small, unseen roles can either be performed by Mackey or another actor.

NOTE FROM THE AUTHOR

This play is built rhythmically; performances should be lively and quick-paced. It is also a very physical show and therein lies much of the humour, particularly in regards to the camel ride, the play within the play and the birth. There are some obscure references to Shakespeare, *The Last of the Mohicans*, *A Christmas Carol* and the Gospel of Luke within the story. It is not at all imperative that the audience be familiar with these references as long as each of the "plays" have a very distinct colour and style to them so that when they are pulled out of the hat altogether they create a ridiculous conglomerate.

The playwright would also like to acknowledge the fact that bits of Joe Mackey's poems are taken from and inspired by *Sawney's Letters and Cariboo Rhymes* by James Anderson, the "Bard of the Cariboo," written between 1863–1871 in Barkerville, BC.

GLOSSARY OF TERMS FOR NON-CANADIANS

THE ART OF DRAMATIC GESTURE (OR GESTICULATION)
A study of specific movements to indicate various states of emotion, used on the Victorian stage.

BC
British Columbia, a colony of England that joined Canada's confederation in 1871.

BUSHWHACKED
Cabin fever, not a lot of contact with people, particularly women.

CANADA
The country north of the United States. In 1870, Canada only consisted of Ontario, Quebec, Nova Scotia and New Brunswick.

CARIBOO
A large cousin of the reindeer, also the name of a region in Northern BC.

CLAIM
In 1870 in the Cariboo, this meant a piece of land, typically 100 feet x 100 feet, allotted to a gold miner for a fee of $5.00 USD.

EH
To be used in place of the American "huh."

GRAMPUS CHASERS
Whalers.

SKOOKUM
Strong.

TOQUE
A woolen skull-hugging cap, rhymes with "fluke."

ACT ONE

In the darkness we hear someone blowing on kindling to make a fire; it catches and crackles in the crisp cold night. We see the fire-lit, dim outline of MACKEY, scratching away with a pen and ink, writing in the last line of his prologue. He is wearing a toque, a dirty pair of red one-piece long johns and big muddy leather boots. His face is boyish and comely and his hair is matted. He has a straggling bit of a beard. His heritage is hard to place, but he's definitely not fully Caucasian. His teeth glint in the light—one tooth is gold; he smiles mischievously to himself, quite pleased with his work. Mules are heard in the background settling down for the evening; perhaps someone in the distance is strumming "The Young Man from Canada" by James Anderson. MACKEY shakes coffee grounds from a canvas pouch into an empty bean tin full of water and extends it over the fire to boil it. He holds the writing paper over the fire to dry the ink, hears a wolf howl in the distance, then reads his rough draft prologue, mostly off book, out to his imaginary audience. His enthusiasm is infectious.

MACKEY:
>It's a silent night in the Cariboo
>As black and cold as my cup.
>I've a Yuletide tale to travel with you
>Down the Fraser and back up.
>
>So grab your bearskins and your boots, be bold
>Cuddle up now don't be shy.
>We've got many miles before we hit gold
>If we don't come close we'll die.
>
>Joe Mackey's my name and I've gained some lore
>As a jack of many trades

I'm a Great Frontier profiteer and your
Canadian chorus … eh?

Now the year is 1870 here
In the gold rush of BC
Still a colony of the Crown I fear
Hoping for confederacy.

Gold fever drew north thousands of miners
From Europe and down under.
Some wild American forty-niners
All of us set to plunder!

Colonial Brits, indentured Chinese
With pack mule guides to lead 'em.
Joined by Natives who survived pox disease,
Black slaves railwayed to freedom.

Now all of us men with our pan and picks
Up the Fraser we did glean.
But when winter hit we froze off our bits
'faint of heart hightailed it clean.

So what we got left is a skookum fleet
Some crazy and some naïve.
Those who love it here call it "sweet home sweet"
The rest are too broke to leave.

But even the brave can't pan in the freeze
When the creek—she ain't swimmin',
We yearn to go south for comfort and ease:
Fresh food, clean sheets and women.

Girls to men: one to sixty. Understood?
Ya gotta court wide and broad.
For a gold rush woman the odds are good
But the goods are usually odd.

Last year I hopped aboard a whaling ship
Docked at a sunny-side port.
I found a hotel where the Scotch was chip
Met a girl I dared to court.

I left her high and dry, back to my claim
To pan off springtime squatters.
But I couldn't stop dreaming of that dame
I met in warmer waters.

Six months later, I'm San Diego bound
To woo her back, wish me luck.
Hope she won't greet me with a rifle round.
Three cheers for the brave Canuck!

MACKEY cheers with his audience, sweeps his arm for the lights. We are transported to FANNY's saloon in sunny San Diego, once elegant, now sparse. There is a sign through the window that reads "Dubeau's New Fashion Saloon and Hotel: World-class Theatre, Dancing Girls, Billiards Room, Fine Ales." Over this sign is a "for sale" sign. FANNY enters from behind the bar, muttering exclamations of frustration, sputtering French oaths and brandishing her fists in a search so heated; she will pop the strings on her corset soon. FANNY is a beautiful woman, albeit somewhat haggard and hard-nosed. Her faded Victorian gown—once brightly coloured and glamorous— still becomes her. She speaks with a slight Parisian accent.

FANNY:
(*under her breath*) Darn the Pageant Player puff puffs! Where are you?! Où êtes vous? Si ils sont parties je les tuerais! Their bags are gone, the room is cleared!

She grabs her rifle from behind the bar and marches throughout the saloon. She approaches a side door, hides the rifle behind her back, composes herself, knocks politely on the door then inquires sweetly.

Monsieur Blake? Are you there with your actors? C'est Madame Dubeau ici … Allo?

She looks in through the door carefully, sees nobody, then stomps.

Maudit! I will pluck every hair from your beard!

She unlocks the front door and cautiously pokes her head

11

outside. She looks up and notices a "for sale" sign boarded over her saloon sign. She gasps with indignation.

How dare the maudit bank! Bordel! Business is bad enough!

FANNY thrusts open the door, rips the "for sale" sign down, brings it into the saloon and jumps on top of it until it is destroyed, leaving the door open.

I am not for sale!

WILLIAM calls out raggedly and falls through the door.

WILLIAM:
Praise the heavens you are open. I desperately need to die!

FANNY:
Reverend! Mon Dieu!

WILLIAM:
My heart is like a chestnut cracked open over the fire of God's wrath!

WILLIAM reels in, reeking, and lands head first onto the floor. FANNY gasps and shuts the door and runs to him with rifle in hand. He is half-dazed with drink and dressed in ratty black Anglican minister vestments. He looks older than he is and has a grizzly beard and spidery thin hair.

FANNY:
Look at you! What are you doing outside?

He rolls over to find the end of her rifle at his nose.

WILLIAM:
(*terrified*) Please don't shoot! Or maybe you should. (*points the rifle to his brain, shuts his eyes and braces himself*) Do it!

FANNY:
This bullet is not for you, it is for Monsieur Blake and the Pageant Players! Pft!

WILLIAM:
(*momentarily distracted*) Actors?

FANNY:

Never trust a man who lies for a living!

WILLIAM:

(*happy thought*) Will there be a show?

FANNY:

No! They escaped!

WILLIAM:

Fie! The blackguards! You don't say, Madame?!

FANNY:

I just said I say! If I had an Appaloosa pony I'd hunt them down and shoot them between the pentameters!

WILLIAM:

(*new thought*) I wager they boarded the ship, and are headed round the cape for England!

FANNY:

England?!

WILLIAM:

A rather large steamer, *The Champion*, sailed off this morning with my official resignation as minister on it.

FANNY:

Did you see them?!

WILLIAM:

No. I was too busy weeping in my own personal purgatory. (*sadly announces*) It is my anniversary today.

FANNY:

(*sudden stop, shocked*) You never told me you were married.

WILLIAM:

To the Church I was, to the Church! I sailed over exactly ten years ago today, to bring the word of the Lord to the wild Californians. Not a single conversion. I am a failed man. Here's my gold cross, Madame, it's all I have left to offer. I wish to drink myself to death before I cause my creator any more disgrace. Please poison me with your sweet fermented hell bound grains and let me die in your alabaster arms ... !

She grabs WILLIAM by the scruff and plunks him on a chair.

FANNY:
(*beat*) No. I cannot afford to bury you. Come and sit, Reverend, you are crumpled like the yesterday news. I'll make us some coffee. It will help us make our world stand up. (*surveys him*) This ... is very terrible evangelism.

WILLIAM:
(*discouraged*) I know. It is a victorious day for the Catholics.

FANNY:
And I do not know why you quit the Church. It is the only business that boom right now with the depression ... zut alors ...

She shakes off his jacket and towels off his head, mothering him.

You are covered with all the damp, petit chou, and will catch the fever around your ears. I believe you were never meant to be a priest ...

His head is toweled right into her bosom; he sighs with bliss.

WILLIAM:
Perhaps you are right ...

FANNY:
(*pushes him off*) Here. You are the most pathetic thing I have seen since my husband, Louis.

FANNY throws him the towel to wipe off his clothes. She sashays around the corner and picks up a pile of letters and starts to sort through her bills with frantic worry.

Bills bills bills! The maudit Pageant Players stiff me for one week room and board and now I have no cat to throw to the mortgage dogs! I should know not to trust the English, no offense.

14

WILLIAM:
    None taken. I do not trust myself.

FANNY:
    (*almost in tears*) The bank will foreclose and sell my saloon
    right under my toes! Everything I work so hard for, William.
    My theatre and my coffin are dead for now good!

WILLIAM:
    No!

FANNY:
    Oui!

    *MACKEY bursts into the saloon, excitedly, well dressed and
    scrubbed. Turns quickly out to the audience.*

MACKEY:
    Recognize me? The Canadian, brave. (*sniffs his armpit*)
    Smellin' like a new plucked rose
    All that it took was a bath and a shave
    Now much improved on the nose.

    (*gives a fellow some advice*) A man must part with his natural oils
    If he wants the girls to blush.
    In order to reap those feminine spoils
    He'll scrub with a firm wire brush.

    (*grandly*) Madame Dubeau?!

FANNY:
    (*suddenly frantic that he's a creditor, runs for her gun*) If you're
    with the bank I'll shoot you off the property!

MACKEY:
    Madame, no, no … I met you last year and auditioned for
    the part of Hamlet! (*recites badly*) To be or not to be!

FANNY:
    (*resolutely deflates him*) Not to be. No offense. But I do not
    hire Chinese or Mexicans or whatever you are. Hamlet was
    the Dane not the darky. Wait for Othello.

WILLIAM:
He looks Russian to me.

MACKEY:
(*hotly*) I'm Canadian.

FANNY gasps, cries with fright and runs to grab her rifle.

FANNY:
CANADIAN?! Mon Dieu!

MACKEY:
(*suddenly frightened*) Pardon? Qu'est-ce que vous avez dit?

FANNY:
Vous parlez français?! That's the proof. You are Canadian for
sure! You bash the brains of babies and you kill good Cora
Monroe!

WILLIAM:
Calm down, Fanny!

MACKEY:
(*bewildered*) I haven't killed anybody … ! I'm a translator in
the mines up north, I speak seven languages—

FANNY:
Do not try to fool me, I know my red men! There's only
two kinds of French-speaking savages: Canadians who are
bad or Mohicans who are good.

MACKEY:
(*hoping she'll put the gun down*) I'm good, I'm good!

FANNY:
If you are Mohican, show me your blue turtle tattoo!

MACKEY:
My name is Joe Mackey …

WILLIAM:
Mackey? That sounds Scottish! Good Lord, that's worse … !

MACKEY:
Not all Canadians are Indians.

WILLIAM:
I think he may be right, Fanny. It has been a while since *The Last of the Mohicans*. I am sure the land is civilized now.

MACKEY:
It's a British colony.

WILLIAM:
God save the queen.

FANNY:
(*puts rifle down*) Pardonnez-moi.

MACKEY:
(*politely*) Pas du tout ...

FANNY:
English, please, my French c'est terrible with all these Yankees twist my ear. I used to speak three languages and now I only speak one: broken Fanny. So what do you want?

MACKEY:
I am looking for one of your performers.

FANNY:
The theatre she is dead. Between Horton's new hotel with the freak show midgets and the bird lady, and the Klondike gold rush emptying the street, there is no one here for the art. Just me and the heathen left.

MACKEY:
What?! Then where's Marta?!

FANNY gasps with recognition.

FANNY:
You?!

WILLIAM:
(*suddenly transported*) Miss Marta Reddy? The Little Treasure?

FANNY:

(*remembering with dread*) I should have known … !

WILLIAM:

(*jumps in*) Alas, Marta vanished. It has left me inconsolable.

WILLIAM begins to weep.

FANNY:

(*put out*) William, please!

MACKEY:

You have no idea where she went?

WILLIAM:

Some say she headed to New York to find a stage worthy of her talent.

FANNY snorts.

FANNY:

The only stage worthy of her talent is the third floor of a melodeon!

MACKEY:

How dare you!

WILLIAM:

She's only thirteen!

FANNY:

Twenty-two!

WILLIAM:

Twenty-two?! But the theatre program said …

FANNY:

She's small, she lie. People like William love the child star, they fancy the baby! Pathétique!

WILLIAM:

(*hotly*) I do not "fancy" her, Madame, I require her! She embodies innocence. Every time I hear her sing I feel redeemed.

FANNY:

Innocence? Bah! I caught them in the dressing room! She carry on illicit with an Eskimo Mongolian celestial slanty half-breed Canadian right here!

She looks MACKEY right in the eye.

MACKEY:

(*angry*) Enough out of you, wench! Just tell me where she is! I'll pay you well. (*offers a fist of money*)

FANNY:

You spit at me with that coloured-man money?! I tell you nothing.

MACKEY:

Fine. I will find her on my own, and then, I will be back to save her reputation!

He turns to go. She snatches the bills then yells after him.

FANNY:

You are the one who ruin her reputation! She's above the seamstress on A Street! See for yourself! You are the devil with the two horns, the two forks and one big trouble! You will get both of you killed!

MACKEY is gone. WILLIAM turns to FANNY.

WILLIAM:

Why did Marta lie about her age?

FANNY:

Women have to lie, William, for men to make them out to be angels.

WILLIAM:

Fanny, I have never seen you turn so mean.

FANNY:

And I have never seen you so liquored!

WILLIAM immediately puts his head down like a kicked dog and FANNY starts wiping tables vigorously in silence.

Zut alors … I am not prejudice, William. I don't care if he's a half-breed stinking whatever. But other people they don't like the Orientals or the darkies. I'm just trying to protect him.

WILLIAM:
He speaks very good English for a Canadian.

FANNY:
Blue Birds do not mate with Pelicans. He is not a proper Christian.

WILLIAM:
(*depressed*) Who is?

FANNY:
He is from a strange people with strange ways.

WILLIAM:
Aye, the Scottish are a funny lot.

FANNY:
No white man is going to let a coloured man take one of the only women around.

WILLIAM:
You're right. Star-crossed lovers. They'll be run out of every town they enter.

FANNY:
Marta always do the opposite of good. Probably why her father sold her.

WILLIAM:
(*incredulous*) Her father sold her?!

FANNY:
Oui. Her father in Germany sold her to be a Hurdy-Gurdy dancer in America. But she got sick on the boat and so the boss dump her at my door. Little Marta. Ten years old, hair fall out in chunks, skinny and small. I did not know if she

would even live. I never feel nothing but business for my dancing girls but this one … this one … like a baby bird that fall out of the nest and you must save it from the dogs. Peep peep with that little stretching hungry neck.

WILLIAM:
Poor girl!

FANNY:
Never mind, she have the silver platter! I taught her English, I gave her singing and acting lessons, I made her into a star! But instead of thanks, she demands to play *my* roles. Zut alors. (*snorts*) Nobody took *me* in like I took her, nobody bought *my* freedom in Paris! (*shudders*) Marrying Louis was the only way to get to the New World.

WILLIAM:
Louis, your late husband?

FANNY:
Oui. God rest his soul the bastard.

WILLIAM:
How were you widowed?

FANNY:
A mining accident.

WILLIAM:
Was there a cave-in?

FANNY:
No, I hit him over the head with a shovel.

WILLIAM:
Good heavens!

FANNY:
He had it coming! I only meant to stun him; it was the fall that actually kill him. Poor Louis. So, I sold his claim in San Francisco, moved here and bought this saloon, and if I lose it then it means his death was all for nothing!

WILLIAM:
Do you think you'll ever marry again, Fanny?

FANNY:
Is that an offer?

WILLIAM:
Well I ...

FANNY:
A woman marries—you get my land, my money, and what do I get?

WILLIAM:
(*somewhat sincere*) My protection?

FANNY:
(*snorts*) Pah!

WILLIAM:
My undying affection? The conjugation of our various ... verbs?

FANNY:
Not an equal trade. Besides, you're married to the Church.

WILLIAM:
(*sinks*) Divorced. The Church does not want me. I have not produced her any children, and I've been sleeping on the sofa for years ...

> *He reaches for the whiskey while there is a knock at the door. FANNY jumps. AMERICAN POST reaches his hand through the mail slot with a registered letter.*

AMERICAN POST:
American Post, ma'am. Registered letter for the Pageant Players.

FANNY:
(*ready to burst into a tirade*) The Pageant Players! (*stops, thinks*) Registered? (*aside, to herself*) Maybe there's money ... (*snatches it*) Merci!

She grabs the letter. The hand withdraws quickly, and she locks the door.

AMERICAN POST:
Hey! I need a signature from Mr. Blake.

FANNY:
Sign this!

FANNY sticks a rifle out the door slot and shoots. AMERICAN POST leaps, yelps and runs away. She reads the envelope while WILLIAM looks out the window to see if AMERICAN POST is all right.

WILLIAM:
Was that necessary?!

FANNY:
Today, oui.

WILLIAM:
Is that a letter for the Pageant Players?

FANNY:
It's mine.

WILLIAM:
Oh, I'm confused. So, it's from the Pageant Players then, to you?

FANNY:
(covering) Sure. Oui.

WILLIAM:
Maybe they sent your rent?

FANNY:
I'm not counting on my chicken eggs for that. *(reads address)* The Theatre Royal, Barkerville, in the colony of British Columbia. Où est ça, where is that?!

WILLIAM:
Columbia? South America, I believe.

FANNY:

Oh! Columbia! Where the coffee is from. (*disengages him from the whiskey and offers him coffee instead*) Have some more!

WILLIAM:

How could they have sent it from Columbia? They just left this morning—

He reaches to look at the address, she snaps it out of sight.

FANNY:

(*snaps*) It is rude to read other people's mail, Monsieur.

WILLIAM:

Forgive me.

FANNY:

Those pompous English puff puffs ...

WILLIAM:

Do you only like the French, Fanny?

FANNY:

Of course not, I cannot stand the French. Why do you think I left Paris?

She rips the letter open and a bunch of money and tickets fall out. FANNY gasps and gathers it up, counts it, then stuffs the money quickly into her bosom before WILLIAM sees it.

(*undertone*) Two hundred dollars! Mon Dieu!

WILLIAM:

What, Fanny?

FANNY:

Nothing. (*reads aloud and gasps*) Ah?! "Dear Pageant Players, the Cariboo Amateur Dramatic Association has agreed to your contract terms to perform the week of Christmas. Enclosed is a per diem for the trip and your pre-paid tickets for the steamer to Fort Yale, and the Barnard's Express to Barkerville ... (*waves tickets excitedly*) Upon completion of your first week of performance you shall receive the amount agreed to of (*gasps, barely whispers the amazing amount of money*) five hundred dollars … "!

WILLIAM:

You're being offered a show in Columbia?

FANNY:

No, not me, the Pageant Players … (*brainstorming and lying at once*) Oui! Oui! Bonne idée, William! (*plans to herself*) The Pageant Players hightailed it back to London, so we … we could replace them! Take the job. But no way to know for sure they're gone, so we'd have to beat them to the chase— (*big gasp, even better!*) We could say we were them! (*announces*) Fanny Dubeau's Pageant Players, an international touring theatre extravaganza!!!

> *Suddenly the door rattles as though it is being pulled open while locked, then gun shots and sound of breaking glass are heard. Startled, FANNY and WILLIAM duck under the table and scream. There is a pounding at the door. A CREDITOR speaks through the door, unseen.*

CREDITOR:

(*shouts threateningly*) Fanny Dubeau, I know you're in there! Your account is now past due!

FANNY:

(*terrified, speaks through the letter slot*) The money is coming!

> *CREDITOR grabs her nose and squishes it through the slot painfully, she squirms and wriggles, down on her knees in pain.*

CREDITOR:

We need it now!

> *FANNY rifles through her bosom, pained and panicked.*

FANNY:

D'accord, d'accord! Oui! Here! Here's two hundred, take it! The rest will come at the end of the month!

> *CREDITOR takes it and releases her nose.*

CREDITOR:
  Nice doing business with you.

  FANNY breathes a sigh of relief and sinks to the floor.

WILLIAM:
  Good Lord, Fanny ...

FANNY:
  We are going to Columbia, so help me, God! I will save my saloon and put red velvet seats and chandeliers! A new blue dress and satin shoes with the bow and the little white buckle of ivory and drink chocolate! Pashoo Louis, roll over in your grave and look at your rocker box now! First the jungles of British Columbia, then New York, then the world! But where am I going to find the actors? I need at least a leading man and an ingénue ...

WILLIAM:
  You're going to do a show?! Just like the good ol' days, grampus chasers wall to wall with Fanny's Frolic and the ringing of the bell!

  WILLIAM starts clapping and stomping and singing out the tune of "Buffalo Gals" while FANNY breaks into a joyful high-kicking dance, hooting and singing.

BOTH:
  Fanny Dubeau won't you come out tonight
  Come out tonight, come out tonight
  Fanny Dubeau won't you come out tonight
  And dance by the light of the moon!

  While they sing, WILLIAM holds FANNY around the waist and she scoots her legs between his and then she is swung up into the air with her feet towards the ceiling ... in theory of course. They end up in each other's arms, laughing. They look into each other's eyes ... There is a moment ... then they quickly separate. WILLIAM clears his throat and FANNY smoothes her skirts. Both are suddenly awkward.

WILLIAM:
Yes, well, yes, right. My apologies for the equilibrium.

FANNY:
Ça va, my bell is harder to ring now. I have not performed since spring! My proportion they turn from ballet to opera.

WILLIAM:
So, what show will you take to Columbia? Everyone loves Charles Dickens!

FANNY:
Yes, but our finest play is my adaptation of *The Last of the Mohicans*.

FANNY suddenly throws herself into a dramatic gesture for a damsel in distress.

FANNY:
(*as Cora Monroe*) What are you looking at, Mohican? Mighty son of the forest?

WILLIAM:
(*as Mohican, with ridiculous "Indian" accent*) I'm looking at you, miss.

FANNY does a faint in full form "Art of Dramatic Gesture."

FANNY:
I could sleep in peace with such a fearless and generous-looking youth for my sentinel!

WILLIAM:
(*as Mohican, proudly grunts*) Huh! (*breaks character*) I never professed to be a great red chief, but a hapless coward, I can relate to ... (*suddenly Hamlet, stabbed and in the throes of death*) Wretched queen, adieu! / Let it be; Horatio, I am dead, / Thou livest, report me and my cause aright / To the unsatisfied.

WILLIAM lies face down in death and FANNY is quite sincerely taken.

27

FANNY:
You are powerful with the words.

WILLIAM:
(*remorsefully, still prostrate*) But never a soul saved. I need a drink.

FANNY:
I need an actor. William, how would you like to do Hamlet in Columbia?

> *Black out. Lights up on MARTA sitting, sewing a quilt that completely obscures her body. MACKEY conspires with audience before he enters, points out MARTA, sees her innocently sewing and is appalled.*

MACKEY:
Marta … ?

See how my star has fallen from the sky!
Darning socks … far from the stage.
This might endear her to my humble pie
Or it may just whet her rage … (*gulp*)

"Was ever woman in this humour wooed?"
'hasn't heard from me since spring.
My knees are knocking and my breath is short
Now where did I put that ring?! (*fumbles, finds it*)

> *MACKEY knocks on the door; MARTA thinks it is the seamstress and doesn't get up.*

MARTA:
Come in, Lottie. I'm just about finished piecing.

> *MACKEY enters.*

MACKEY:
Miss Marta Reddy?

> *MARTA's back stiffens immediately when she hears his voice; she pulls the quilt higher. She has a slight German accent.*

MARTA:
Who's there?

MACKEY:
Mr. Joe Mackey, miss.

MARTA:
(shocked gasp) Joe! *(speechless)*

MACKEY:
I ... I ... wrote you a little poem ... I ... *(fumbles with his papers, begins to recite, half by memory, nervous but sincere)*

I once knew a girl with raven black hair,
Her skin was fair and— *(interrupted)*

MARTA:
(controlled) I don't want to hear your fancy words. Where have you been?

MACKEY:
Up north.

MARTA:
So why'd you come back?

MACKEY:
To ... to ...

MARTA:
Spit it out!

MACKEY:
To ask you to marry me.

MACKEY holds out his hand with a ring, holds his breath anxiously awaiting her answer. MARTA still has her back to him.

MARTA:
(coldly) Mr. Mackey, after careful consideration, I have decided to accept your proposal of marriage.

MARTA stands up solemnly. MACKEY and everyone else realizes for the first time that MARTA is seven months pregnant. MACKEY's eyes pop out of his head. He does a quick aside to the audience.

MACKEY:

A man could respond in more ways than one
My first thought was simply, "Run!"

She grabs the ring and he bolts out the door in sheer fright. She yells after him, holding up the ring.

MARTA:

I'll see you in church or I'll see you in court!

MARTA races after him, as best as she can. Lights change. Back to FANNY and WILLIAM. FANNY is finishing writing a letter.

FANNY:

... we should arrive in Barkerville by the middle of December. Thank you, Mr. Bowron. Sincerely, Fanny Dubeau (*whispers*) alias George Blake, The Pageant Players.

FANNY puts down her pen, stuffs an envelope with the paper.

Voilà! (*goes to the door, shouts*) American Post?!

AMERICAN POST's hand pokes through the crack in the door and snatches the letter.

AMERICAN POST:

Don't shoot!

FANNY closes the door.

FANNY:

Bon! Good! Done! (*turns to WILLIAM*) Do you think it will be hot in British Columbia? What do you suppose they have for food down there besides coffee? Maybe bananas? Maybe monkey brains ... ?!

WILLIAM:

(*panicking*) Fanny, I'm flattered by the offer, but I cannot grace the stage. You need to find a real actor. (*despairing*) I am a neophyte with histrionics—!

FANNY:
Whatever you said, I do not know. Tu serais fantastique! I need you. All my men went to the Klondike, Lizzie got married, the twins went east ... there is no time for auditions ... !

WILLIAM:
What about Miss Marta Reddy?

FANNY:
Impossible!

MACKEY bursts into the saloon again and searches wildly for WILLIAM.

MACKEY:
Is the reverend still here? Thank God! We need to talk!

FANNY:
It is the Canadian.

MACKEY runs to WILLIAM and buries his head by WILLIAM's feet. They both look at him for a moment.

WILLIAM:
You found Marta.

MACKEY:
(*despairing*) Yes. I'm afraid! I don't know what to do, I ...

FANNY:
Up, up, Mr. Mackey. (*lifts him onto a chair, taking pleasure in mocking him*) Have a coffee before you start defending her honor, it is on the house. It is Columbian. (*pours him one, then winks at WILLIAM*) Pure *British* Columbian!

MACKEY:
(*looks up, oddly*) You get it shipped down?

FANNY:
You mean up. Columbia is south, oui?

MACKEY:
Down. *British* Columbia's north.

31

FANNY / WILLIAM:
What?!

FANNY:
Ciel! Are you sure?!

WILLIAM:
How *far* north?

MACKEY:
Sort of under Alaska.

FANNY / WILLIAM:
UNDER ALASKA?!

FANNY:
(*opens the door and runs out, shouting*) AMERICAN POST?!

WILLIAM reaches for his flask, MACKEY notices.

MACKEY:
I'll take some Scotch.

WILLIAM pours MACKEY a huge Scotch and puts a bunch into his own coffee.

WILLIAM:
So, you are a Scottish Canadian living with the Columbian Spaniards under British rule up in the Arctic? (*utterly confounded*) Why?!

FANNY enters, horrified.

FANNY:
Too late! The letter is gone! Qu'est-ce que j'ai fait?

MACKEY:
Will you hear a confession?

WILLIAM:
No, no ... I have given up the cloth.

MACKEY:
I don't know why I ran, I just ... panicked! What am I going

to do? We can't travel to the Cariboo with a newborn, and I'll lose my claim if we stay here!

FANNY:

The Cariboo?! (*reads the envelope*) Ever hear of the Barkerville Theatre Royal?

MACKEY:

(*impatient*) Yes. (*carries on with his grief*) Imagine what Marta's been going through, alone all this time expected a child? You'll have to marry us right away. Will you do that, Reverend?

WILLIAM:

I cannot.

MACKEY:

Why?

FANNY:

Because this reverend will not be doing any Far East oogily boogily ceremony or none of that Confucius Buddha bar mitzvah hoodoo. Who *do* you believe in, anyway?

MACKEY:

Calvin, I'm a Presbyterian. Who do *you* believe in?

FANNY:

Nobody! I am a Christian! I do not believe in anything, which is more than I can say for you! I bet you are not even baptized!

WILLIAM:

Of course he is if he's a Presbyterian!

MACKEY:

(*realizing*) Actually, no, I don't think I was baptized ...

FANNY:

Well if you are not baptized you will go to hell HELL HELL! And even worse, no decent reverend will marry you!

MACKEY:

(*getting even more worried*) We have to get married!

WILLIAM:

Nothing much to baptism, Joe. A chap could do it right
here if he wanted. The first and only baptism I did was
when I was ten years old. Baptized Rufus, a wonderful
German Shepherd ...

> *MACKEY is sincerely taken in with the idea but the reverend is
> not serious at all.*

MACKEY:

What does baptizing do?

WILLIAM:

(*romanticizes*) It makes you a child of God, and then you
belong to the family of the Church forever ... (*a moment of
gloom*) Or some such.

MACKEY:

(*taken with the idea*) A child of God. Sounds all right. If that's
what it takes. (*decides*) What do I have to say?

WILLIAM:

(*dismissively*) Come on now, Joe. I would have to ask you to
renounce all sinful desires ...

MACKEY:

I'll try.

> *MACKEY pushes his Scotch aside, WILLIAM takes it as an
> offer and downs it.*

WILLIAM:

Accept Christ as your saviour ...

MACKEY:

Done.

FANNY:

Baptizing will not make you white!

MACKEY:

Quiet!

WILLIAM:

(not even paying attention) And fuss and nonsense, what is
the rest? I guess, hmm, the reverend would say, oh ... heavens,
I have to think back to seminary now ... having never
accomplished a bloody conversion, never a soul saved, I don't
remember the order of things! Oh yes, that your whole trust
is in His grace and love, follow and obey, and that whole
business.

FANNY:

(realizes this may work to her advantage) Never a soul saved ...

WILLIAM:

(trying to recall the process) But all you really need is immersion
in water.

MACKEY:

That's it?

FANNY:

Just water?

WILLIAM:

I say: (blesses MACKEY) I baptize you in the name of the
Father, and of the Son, and of the Holy Spirit. Amen.

*MACKEY realizes he's just been baptized. FANNY thinks fast,
offers MACKEY a pitcher of water and he dumps it over his
own head.*

MACKEY:

Done! Wahoo!

FANNY:

Well, Reverend, looks like you just saved yourself a soul.

WILLIAM:

(realizes) What? Impossible!

MACKEY:

(shakes his head) One sacrament down, one more to go! Yeah!
I feel like a new man.

WILLIAM:

Good Lord!

FANNY:

Now will you do Hamlet?!

MACKEY:

Hamlet?

WILLIAM:

(*thrilled*) What a piece of work is a man!

WILLIAM and MACKEY embrace.

MACKEY:

I'm going to go get Marta so you can marry us right away! Whew! I'm on a roll!

WILLIAM:

(*great new idea*) Fanny, you could cast Marta and Joe in your play! She'd be respectable now.

MACKEY:

You need an actor?

FANNY:

Marta maybe, but I would never even *think* of casting this muddy man mutt!

MACKEY:

(*angrily*) What do you know of who I am?!

FANNY:

I know that the audience will boo an Oriental Italian off the stage because your blood stink and you are half a man!

MACKEY suddenly gets an idea, stands very still, then lets out a blood-curdling "Indian" war whoop and leaps onto the bar behind FANNY and grabs her hair as if he will scalp her. She screams. He shouts out the few words he knows in Chinook, as though he was making a grand announcement declaring his proud lineage. The others, shocked, don't know the difference.

MACKEY:

Ab'ba, okoke tyee potlatch dolla, konaway siwash mokst
dolla Boston illahie konaway week!

*MACKEY throws FANNY by the hair across the bar room, she
falls to her knees. WILLIAM skitters away in fright.*

WILLIAM:

What did he say?!

FANNY:

I do not know. Something in Indian I think!

*MACKEY does another war whoop and leaps closer to FANNY.
She screams and cowers.*

MACKEY:

Mesika momook kunamokst okoke kawkawak man kopa
tahtlum pe mokst dingding shut!

FANNY:

(*eyes closed in fear, shouts*) William, grab his tomahawk!

MACKEY:

(*declares proudly*) Mesika mamook sinamoxt sun week koshe
spose okoke illahee hyas cole! (*switches over to Chinese dialect,
during which he circles her, almost transfixing her with slow martial
arts moves*) Nai dei ng dei tui or hai ai sui? Or ng hai fa guo
nin, or yiu ng hai gwei lo, or wat che hai hong nin, or yit
ding hai ga na dai nin! (*over to French*) Je suis du Canada!
(*switches over to English with a pseudo-Indian accent*) I am a
child of God, the last of the Mohicans!

*FANNY gasps in shock and sudden frightened admiration as
though she was looking upon the face of God.*

FANNY:

If you are Mohican, show me your blue turtle tattoo!

*This suddenly takes MACKEY aback; at the same time,
WILLIAM understands what he is up to. They lock eyes.
MACKEY grabs FANNY by the hair again and drags her*

across the floor with a "whoop" while she kicks and screams. Meanwhile, WILLIAM takes FANNY's ink bottle, presses a sheet of paper down on the rim, rips MACKEY's shirt open and presses the sheet of paper onto his bare chest, making a blue ink circle imprint, all unseen by the kicking proprietor. MACKEY throws FANNY with a roar, and she rolls to the other end of the saloon floor.

FANNY:
How dare you!

MACKEY rips his shirt open quickly to expose the tattoo.

MACKEY:
Woman! Behold!

FANNY gasps with realization and faints. WILLIAM is shocked too, and rushes over to MACKEY whispering.

WILLIAM:
Are you really Mohican?

MACKEY:
(*whispers back, devilishly pleased*) No. But I read the book.

WILLIAM:
(*delighted at the ruse*) Well done, sir, well done! She is sure to hire you now!

MARTA suddenly waddles in, huffing and puffing angrily. She sees MACKEY with his shirt open, holding FANNY in a somewhat romantic-looking position. MACKEY drops the dead weight and covers his chest.

MACKEY:
Marta!

WILLIAM is shocked.

WILLIAM:
The child … is with child?!

MARTA screams out like a petulant infant.

MARTA:
I AM NOT A CHILD!

This suddenly wakens FANNY. MACKEY moves to pull out a chair for MARTA.

MACKEY:
Sit down, Marta …

MARTA:
(*blubbers proudly in German*) Ich bin kein Kind, ich bin eine starke deutsche Frau!

FANNY:
(*groggy, coming to*) Marta …?!

MARTA pulls MACKEY's ear till he's on his knees in pain.

MARTA:
Scoundrel! We have a contract!

MACKEY:
I wasn't going anywhere!

MARTA:
Bollocks!

MARTA turns and sees the reverend for the first time, really.

Reverend …

She is suddenly ashamed, lets go of MACKEY's ear.

You shouldn't see me this way.

MARTA bursts into tears.

WILLIAM:
(*awkwardly trying to hide his disillusion*) No matter, Marta, no matter …

MARTA:
(*pointing to MACKEY*) It's all his fault!

MACKEY:

I—

FANNY:

(*interrupts*) Unworthy girl of such noble seed!

MARTA:

Noble seed?! You're the one who told me I had to give up the baby or be out on the streets!

FANNY falls contrite at MACKEY's feet.

FANNY:

I only did what any decent mother would have done! But please forgive me, great chief! I didn't know her child was of such precious lineage!

MARTA:

Great chief?

MACKEY:

Nothing.

MARTA suddenly grabs MACKEY's ear again, then speaks to WILLIAM.

MARTA:

Reverend, can you quickly and legally bind me to this man?

WILLIAM:

Well ...

MARTA:

Then can you get a rope and tie him up till I can find a legitimate parson?

MACKEY:

I'm not going anywhere!

MARTA:

Liar! Liar! Liar!

FANNY:

Marta, sit down in your condition ...

MARTA:

(*barks*) Don't mother me! This is *my* wedding and I'll do it the way I please!

FANNY:

Impudent wench! If you do not calm down I will withdraw my offer to you!

MARTA:

The last "offer" you gave me was the end of your pointed boot!

FANNY:

(*forced kindness*) That was then, this is now.

MARTA:

That then is this now as it ever once was, Fanny!

ALL:

Huh?

MARTA:

Be useful and get me a drink. Make it a double. I'm drinking for two. (*notices MACKEY*) Why is your head wet?

MACKEY:

I was baptized.

WILLIAM:

Fanny, are you offering them roles on the stage?!

FANNY:

Oui! (*aside to WILLIAM*) Imagine, a real Mohican! (*announces*) We will take our rep to the Theatre Royal in the Cariboo to perform the week of Christmas. All of our transportation is paid for (*shows them the tickets*) and we will get ... (*decides to be cheap*) fifty dollars apiece after the show.

MACKEY:

(*impressed*) Fifty dollars?!

FANNY:

But we must leave tonight!

MARTA:

Are you hysterical? If you haven't noticed, I'm seven months pregnant!

FANNY:

Shh! That vulgar word!

MACKEY:

(*starting to worry*) She's right, the journey's three weeks.

FANNY:

When people hear you are married to Marta, they will hate you, sell you nothing, live on the street. They don't honour your kind like I do. We have to take you back to where you came from. Back north in the woods. That is your only chance.

MACKEY:

You're right.

FANNY:

William owes me this much and as for me, I keep the theatre alive!

WILLIAM:

It might just be the better life we're looking for ...

MARTA:

Do I get to play Ophelia?

FANNY:

But ...

MARTA:

OPHELIA!

FANNY:

(*painful agreement*) Oui.

MARTA:

Agreed then.

MACKEY:
Are you sure?

MARTA:
I AM ALWAYS SURE!

They put their hands in for a group pact.

FANNY:
Agreed?

WILLIAM / MACKEY/ MARTA:
Agreed.

WILLIAM:
Let's off to the chapel! My keys have been rescinded but I think I can squirrel us in through the back window!

Black out.

End of Act One.

ACT TWO

Black out. Lights up. Everyone is on the deck of a steamer, dressed in warmer clothing, surrounded by bags, costumes and props. MARTA has some semblance of a wedding dress still on. FANNY reads her scripts. WILLIAM plays a tin whistle. MARTA stares somberly at a map, then into the horizon, then throws up for the hundredth time.

MACKEY:
We married that night, gathered up, went forth.
And to San Francisco, sailed.
Juan de Fuca then, Straight of Georgia, North
Fraser River to Fort Yale.

WILLIAM whistles the ship's arrival and they get off board. FANNY kisses the ground. They pack up their bags and walk. MARTA separates from them and looks around her in wonder.

FANNY:
Mon Dieu, solid ground!

WILLIAM:
(*with interest*) Fort Yale!

MARTA:
Fresh air.

MACKEY:
Not much further now. Just 380 more miles to go. Uphill.

WILLIAM / FANNY:
What?!

MACKEY:
The Hudson's Bay Company is beside the Barnard's Express.
Better buy some decent men's boots.

FANNY:
Pourquoi?

MACKEY:
(*laughs at her high-heeled lace-up boots*) You can't walk in these ridiculous little things, you'll freeze!

FANNY:
WALK?!

MACKEY:
By next week with the altitude it'll be about forty below, with thirty-foot snow drifts. When the team of horses gets stuck we'll have to follow on foot.

WILLIAM:
(*terrified*) This is not a time to joke, Mr. Mackey. Do not scare the women!

MACKEY:
No joke. We're going as high as those mountains over there.

FANNY:
Mon Dieu. No wonder the Pageant Players gave up the contract.

WILLIAM:
Note to the Church of England: Hell indeed freezes over.

FANNY:
I was built for Paris not the Pole! I cannot survive!

MACKEY:
You could stay here, but all you have is a roadhouse filled with bushwhacked miners who haven't seen a woman since August.

WILLIAM:
Barkerville is civilized, you say?

MACKEY:
Relatively.

FANNY:

(whimpers) Will it have hot chocolate, brave Mohican?

MACKEY:

For a price.

WILLIAM:

Then it will be better society for a lady if we keep on. How long till we get there?

MACKEY:

I'm guessing two weeks.

WILLIAM and FANNY sigh in despair. Meanwhile MARTA has been looking around her, enraptured.

MARTA:

It's so beautiful here. I haven't seen mountains since Fichtelgebirge, in der Nähe meines Heims in Deutschland, mit all den Kiefern ... I half expect to see my mother come walking out from those trees ... wo sind Sie jetzt Mutter? Everything smells like pine and wood smoke. It's so white ... so pure. *(proudly, through tears)* Ich bin eine starke deutsche Frau! I am made for the snow!

MACKEY:

Ich bin froh, daß Du es magst.

MARTA:

And to think in those mountains there's nobody around for miles and miles ...

WILLIAM:

(leery) Nobody we wish to meet, that is ...

FANNY pulls out a rifle from a properties bag.

FANNY:

Do not worry, William. I have La Longue Carabine!

MACKEY:

Put that rifle away!

FANNY:
Why?

MACKEY:
We're not in America anymore; it's illegal to have firearms in town.

FANNY:
How am I supposed to protect myself?

MACKEY:
You won't have to. It's too cold up here to make trouble. Come.

> *Lights change. FANNY and WILLIAM pull out clothing and costumes and layer them on, including big men's boots for the women. MACKEY puts his toque on MARTA's head and they board the Barnard's Express coach.*

MACKEY:
We made our way to the Barnard's Express
Caught the next sleigh heading north.
The four-horse stage loaded up all our mess
And our ragtag troupe went forth.

We stopped at the roadhouses when we could
The rest we camped on the way.
Dug out the runners, and walked through the woods,
While rehearsing all our plays.

> *They all bounce in the coach, bundled up, trying to keep warm. FANNY pulls out her scripts.*

FANNY:
Ecoutez, I have the final casting done. There's only four of us, so we have to be inventive. First the Shakespeare. Mr. Teller, who would you like to play in Denmark?

WILLIAM:
(*assuming Hamlet is his*) Besides the title role? Hm ... well, Claudius the King, or Polonius. A torture to decide.

FANNY:

You can play them both and I'll throw in Horatio.

WILLIAM:

Extravagant honour!

FANNY:

I will play Gertrude and Laertes. I've always wanted to do a sword fight. Now, Mrs. Mackey, you will play the ghost, we only have to see your head so we can hide your ... *(seeking word for belly)* disgrace. But as for Ophelia, this is my suggestion. Soyez debout.

MARTA stands. FANNY, while balancing, grabs MARTA's hoopskirt and yanks it up so that it is under MARTA's armpits.

FANNY:

Instead of fair Ophelia, you will be fat Ophelia. Voila.

MARTA pulls her skirts down indignantly.

MARTA:

I can't be fat Ophelia! That's ridiculous.

WILLIAM:

Does not Hamlet foretoken: "as your daughter may conceive, friend look to't?"

MARTA:

She could be fully plucked.

FANNY:

It is very risqué ...

MACKEY:

But possible.

FANNY:

Leave me to consider. And Hamlet ... goes to the Canadian Prince!

WILLIAM:

WHAT?! But you promised me ...

FANNY:
You're too long in the teeth.

MACKEY:
(*very excited, bloodthirsty, holding the skull*) At last, poor Yorick, I slew him, Horatio—a fellow of insolent jest!

WILLIAM:
(*horrified by the interpretation*) Angels and ministers of grace, defend us!

MACKEY:
(*sheepishly*) It's been a while since I've seen it ...

WILLIAM:
Such a horrid execution of the lines! And his "H's" are clearly at a discount! (*undertone*) Fanny, he is obviously miscast ...

FANNY:
We will work on it. Oration is in his blood. Somewhere. Now, Mr. Teller, I also want you to play Rosencrantz and Guildenstern.

WILLIAM:
How am I to play Rosencrantz *and* Guildenstern?

FANNY:
Mon Dieu, I give the man the crown and half the play and he still complains! Now, for *Last of the Mohicans* ... I will play the dark-haired beauty: Cora Monroe. Mr. Mackey will play ... the young Mohican that Cora loves ... (*transported by the thought for a minute*) Mrs. Mackey will play my sister, Alice ... s'il vous plaît, Alice needs to be virtuous. Let us make her fat Alice?

MARTA:
(*resigned*) Fine.

FANNY:
Mr. Teller, you will play Hawk-eye, Duncan, Magua, the Indians, the French and the entire English army.

WILLIAM:

But …

FANNY:

Never argue with the director! (*silence*) Fanny's Frolic is
basically a showcase pour moi. Learn these songs and I will
choreograph once we get there. Finally, *A Christmas Carol.*
Mr. Mackey, you will play Cratchit and young Scrooge. Mrs.
Mackey, you will play Tiny Tim … we will make you
bedridden. I will write in a scene …

WILLIAM:

Forgive us, Charles Dickens!

FANNY:

I will play the other women and Mr. Teller …

WILLIAM:

(*fearful*) Yes?

FANNY:

This will be an easy show for you. You will play Scrooge,
turkey boy, the orphans and all the Cratchit children. William?

WILLIAM:

(*resigned*) Wretched queen.

FANNY:

(*hands out various scripts to each*) Bon. Here is *Mohicans* for
you, *Carol* for you, *Hamlet* for you. Memorize your parts
then switch.

WILLIAM:

Will we not rehearse?!

FANNY:

Pfft! Rehearsals are for amateurs. It is all about the language,
mes amis. The movements will all come natural to you once
we have an audience.

WILLIAM:

(*stands, declaring wildly*) I need to rehearse or I will not do the
plays!

The horses come to a halt, everyone is jolted by the sudden stop. MACKEY stands to ascertain the situation.

MACKEY:

Looks like we didn't quite make it to Spence's Bridge. We're camping here for the night.

FANNY:

Here?! In the middle of nowhere?!

MARTA:

Good. My bladder is bursting.

FANNY:

Taisez-vous! The men do not want to hear your bodily functions! Be a lady.

MARTA:

Piss off!

MARTA exits, smugly pleased. FANNY gasps, indignant. They disembark. The ladies head off into the bush while MACKEY starts a fire. WILLIAM pulls a flask out, takes a swig. MACKEY speaks to him confidentially.

MACKEY:

How do you like the mountains, Reverend?

WILLIAM:

Freezing to death in one's sleep would be peaceful at least. (*beat*) When we get to civilization, you should confirm your vows with a fully ordained minister—my services are suspect.

MACKEY:

Well, I figure the Lord will honour our sacraments, even if the Church doesn't.

WILLIAM:

Quite. If the Lord lived by the Church's honour, I think I would hang myself.

MACKEY:

You don't sound like you put much faith in the institution.

WILLIAM:

Faith in the Church? No. (*gets up*) Love? Yes. I love her, I just cannot live with her. But ooh ... we had our moments. Always was transported by her music and the beautiful words of grace echoing up the steeple. Especially fond of Christmas with candles and carols and pine around the advent wreath. Stained glass apostles throwing their colour gently across the neck of young Sara on the piano. I did feel the divine then ... I did, in England. Surrounded by all that ancient beauty. But ten years here in the New World, tailings with mud-heaped towns, every tree chopped for timbers, desperate men down in the deeps so long their feet rot with gum boot gout. Rather kills the romance. I could not bring any of the beauty to them, only the rules.

MACKEY:

(*looks around him, wonders*) You don't find the beauty here?

WILLIAM:

(*walks into the woods*) Stave off the wolves, will you?

MACKEY:

Where you going?

WILLIAM:

To desecrate a snow bank.

> WILLIAM *wobbles off into the darkness humming "Come Thou Fount." Lights dim. MARTA returns alone and finds MACKEY starting a fire.*

MARTA:

Fanny won't leave me alone! She's obsessed with the baby! I was trying to find a little place in the woods to squat ... but she demanded to keep vigil over the "sacred papoose"! What is that about?! Why is she so fond of you all of a sudden? Last year she couldn't stand the sight of you. Called you a half-breed.

MACKEY:

(*chuckles*) I told her I was the last of the Mohicans.

MARTA:

(*incredulous*) Mohican?! Really?! And she fell for it?

MACKEY:

Vollständig.

MARTA:

Well, that explains why she gawks at you all the time! Narr.

MACKEY:

You jealous?

MARTA:

(*snorts*) Pah! I just can't stand her mooning. You should tell her the truth.

MACKEY:

Maybe it is the truth.

MARTA:

Bollocks. Your name is Joe, not Natty Bumppo.

MACKEY:

All I know is I was found wrapped up in a Hudson's Bay blanket outside the Perth orphanage in an empty whiskey crate.

MARTA:

But with the last name "Mackey," your father must have been Scottish or something.

MACKEY:

No. All the orphans were named "Mackey" after the head matron.

MARTA:

So you have no idea what you are?

MACKEY:

My guess? An unhappy bride ship wife had a dalliance with a Chinese mercantile owner. Or a miner had a bush wife. I don't know. I've traveled east to west looking for a face I resemble ... each language I learn ... I wait to hear something in my heart leap out and say "I'm a child of this tongue" … but it doesn't happen. I'm just a smattering of this and that. It makes me hard to place.

MARTA:

Maybe it is best not to know. I was sold by my father for the worth of a horse. Some heritage for our child. You are from Canada. I'm from Germany. That is enough for people to know. Don't make things worse by pretending to be something you're not.

MACKEY:

If I didn't lie to Fanny about being Mohican, I would never have a chance to act. To walk on the stage as a son, a lover, a prince. For once. To be a part of it all. Do you know what that means? I promise I'll tell her the truth after the show. (*beat*) You warm enough?

MARTA:

I'm afraid the baby will freeze right through my skin.

MACKEY:

The fire will take any second.

MARTA:

He's moving again. Probably trying to keep warm.

MACKEY:

May I?

MACKEY leans in slowly, carefully, towards her belly. She pushes him off roughly.

MARTA:

Don't touch me!

He backs off.

MACKEY:

You keep calling him a he.

MARTA:

I had a dream it was a he.

She thinks better of letting him near her and pulls him in
roughly and plunks his ear to her belly.

There. Now you can try. Now he's moving.

MACKEY speaks to the baby, very tenderly, calls.

MACKEY:
Hello baby.

MACKEY stays where he is and rests his head against her belly,
listening.

MARTA:
When I first started to show, Fanny kept trying to slip
Pennyroyal into my tea. But I refused to lose him. I don't
care if I end up at the melodeon. He's mine, all mine, and
nobody is taking him away from me.

MACKEY:
Don't worry. Nobody's going to take him. *(beat)* He'll be my
first blood relative.

MARTA:
(pause, then snorts) This is the first time we've been alone
since your proposal. What a honeymoon! Hardly makes me
feel wed.

MACKEY:
(a little smile) We aren't officially married until we
consummate ...

MARTA:
(snaps) I'm seven months three feet wide and two hundred
miles not in the mood!

MACKEY:
Of course not! We ... we have lots of time to work things
out between us before we have to think about ... that.

MARTA:
(bolts up again, deciding to address things) Every time I look in
your face, I can't believe it's you.

He changes the subject.

MACKEY:
Need another blanket?

MARTA awkwardly rolls into her sleeping blankets.

MARTA:
No.

MACKEY:
What should we name him?

MARTA:
Something plain.

MACKEY:
I have a feeling he'll become ... a powerful man someday.

MARTA:
(*guarded*) He'll be a half-breed and lucky to find a job.

MACKEY:
It's a different world up north, Marta. Half the population's Chinese. Negroes run shops right in the middle of town, women own gold mines ...

MARTA:
They only tolerate you because they need you!

MACKEY:
The same could be said for our marriage.

MARTA:
(*taken aback*) I thought you said you loved me?!

FANNY breaking in on the argument out of necessity to keep warm and get under her blankets.

FANNY:
Bonjour! Ah, my bearskin is a welcoming sight tonight! Got the fire going, Mr. Mackey?

MARTA:
(*speaking of their love*) Apparently not!

FANNY:
(*to MACKEY*) How do your people start fires?

MACKEY:
Sulfur match.

FANNY:
(*disappointed*) Oh. Not so much traditional. Don't lose touch with the old ways of your people, Joe. You can pass them on to your child. Be proud of who you are.

MARTA:
Never a moment alone.

WILLIAM enters shivering, a pipe lit, and scoots under his blanket.

WILLIAM:
Brrrrrr! I would not be surprised if the horses freeze standing up tonight!

FANNY:
Mon Dieu! What a thinking!

MARTA:
May I have a puff of your pipe, Mr. Teller?

WILLIAM:
Certainly, Mrs. Mackey.

MARTA:
Relaxes the baby.

She takes a big drag.

FANNY:
Well, I say we should have a little bedtime *Hamlet*.

WILLIAM:
A little camp-fire ghost story of the Danish apparition?

FANNY:
All memorized?

They grunt in agreement.

FANNY:
Bon. Where did we leave off?

MARTA:
(*impatient, as Ophelia*) My lord, as I was sewing in my closet, Lord Hamlet with his doublet all unbraced, no hat upon his head, his stocking fouled ... etc., etc.—he comes before me.

WILLIAM:
(*as Polonius*) Mad for thy love?

MARTA:
My lord, I do not know, But truly I do fear it.

WILLIAM:
What said he?

MARTA:
(*goes on a sudden passionate rant, as herself, mixing up the scene with her own love life, almost in one breath*) He said nothing! You know why? Because when it comes down to it, he doesn't really *love* her, he only "tolerates" her! Stupid Hamlet. (*swats MACKEY*)

MACKEY:
What did she expect him to say?!

MARTA:
He could have offered her an explanation! Hamlet heads off to ... England, just disappears one day. Gone! Was he angry, what had she done? Was he in trouble? She didn't know. Two weeks pass, is he dead?! She hopes not to hear he'd been caught under a wheel or drowned off the docks ... and when Ophelia realized she was with child she hoped in vain that Hamlet had gone up north again to find work in the mines and would send for her. But no, not a word. Not

58

even one of his dumb little poems! Indeed, she'd started to believe that he left her *because* of the child. And as it grew bigger, her heart grew smaller, squeezed tight and black like a little piece of coal.

MACKEY:
So Ophelia's love for Hamlet is dead? Is that what you're saying?

MARTA:
She wishes it was! Her memories are a torture! The words of love he whispered to her in the wee hours of the morning, when everyone else slept, and she was there in his arms believing everything was possible ... "My Lord I have remembrances of yours, / That I have longed long to re-deliver!" No wonder Ophelia went MAD AS A HATTER!

She flops down in a huff. WILLIAM gives her the pipe again, not sure what to say. She takes another puff.

MACKEY:
I'm sorry, Marta ... Hamlet didn't know she was with child ...!

MARTA:
That's because Hamlet didn't leave a forwarding address.

She hands back the pipe.

FANNY:
Don't paraphrase the Shakespeare, Marta. It upset the iambic.

FANNY blows out the light and she and WILLIAM roll over. MACKEY whispers to MARTA.

MACKEY:
I thought it would be best if you ... forgot me.

MARTA:
Then why'd you come back?

MACKEY:
I can't live without you.

Silence. They both lie down again.

Take more of this blanket.

MARTA:
Save some for yourself.

MACKEY:
Take it!

MARTA:
(*blasts*) How stupid of you to think that leaving me alone would be better! I would *never* leave *my* baby in a whiskey crate no matter what colour he is! I don't care who does what to me or thinks whatever they might! Your mother was a coward and I am not! And if you leave me again I will hunt you down and kill you.

Silence.

MACKEY:
You gonna be warm enough?

MARTA:
Yeah.

They settle in to sleep. Lights dim. MACKEY pops his head up, pulls out his book of writings, pens something briefly, then narrates under the light of the moon.

MACKEY:
Down the Wagon Road, we sledded along
Snowshoed uphill single file.
Blisters on our feet, Shakespeare on our tongue
Learning our lines by the mile.

At night we'd rest at a road-house or best
Under skies stretched wide and far.
A little frozen Magi briefly blessed
With a glimpse of the North Star.

MACKEY closes his book. MARTA lifts her head to see if FANNY and WILLIAM are asleep. They are. She sits up.

MACKEY and MARTA stare at each other for a moment, then they kiss, passionately, and fall back under the covers. Later, just as the sun starts to light the snow, we see an outline of our hibernating huddle. A wolf bays in the distance. FANNY rolls over, grumbles, then bolts up, her eyes shut tight, and screams. WILLIAM bolts upright too, but his pillow is frozen to the side of his face.

FANNY:
 I cannot see! I cannot see!

MARTA:
 Why not?

WILLIAM:
 What? Hey ... get ... get off! My pillow froze to my whiskers!

MACKEY:
 Here.

MACKEY rips the pillow off the side of WILLIAM's face and takes a few whiskers along with it.

WILLIAM:
 Ouch! I will not have to shave for a month now!

FANNY:
 My eyelashes are frozen together! Au secours! I cannot open my eyes!

WILLIAM:
 Here.

He starts breathing on her eyes to melt the ice.

FANNY:
 What are you doing?

WILLIAM:
 I am melting the ice with my breath.

FANNY:
 William, you could melt Antarctica with that breath. Pardonnez-moi, but I would rather be blind.

MACKEY:

Just put your hands up to your eyelashes, that will melt them.

FANNY:

I am telling you, these conditions are not for the human!

MACKEY:

You need to snuggle in, that's why you're so cold.

FANNY:

I am a respectable woman, Mr. Mackey. I do not snuggle!

MACKEY:

Fine, freeze to death then. Good night.

They all lie down again, MACKEY and MARTA snuggle together, then WILLIAM snuggles up to them, then FANNY snuggles up right in the middle of the huddle.

FANNY:

Ça va, ça va …

WILLIAM:

Watch the boots, ouch!

FANNY:

Sorry. Oooh …

She rubs her side.

WILLIAM:

Do you have a sore back?

FANNY:

Oui. I feel like ten oxen stampede over my back sleeping on the ground like a dog. What I would not do for my feather tic.

WILLIAM:

(*awkwardly*) Perhaps you would be more comfortable if you refrained from sleeping in your various female contraptions, if you do not mind my saying.

FANNY:

William, are you trying to get me out of my corset? Mon Dieu! No decent woman sleep without the underpinning!

MARTA:

No decent woman sleeps. I always take mine off.

FANNY:

Exactement. And look what that got you!

MARTA:

Fanny, don't be such a stubborn fool. You have so many clothes on, nobody's gonna know the difference anyway. Now you men, turn your backs and don't look. Fanny, undo yourself. I have some salve for rheumatic joints. I'll rub some on.

FANNY hides in the blankets and loosens all her clothing so that MARTA can reach the back lacings on her corset.

FANNY:

No really, Marta, Je ne peux pas. I can't.

MARTA:

Just loosen it!

FANNY:

I never take it off. It holds me together.

MARTA:

I don't suppose you bathe with it?

FANNY:

Cette question very personal with men in the earshot!

WILLIAM:

Nobody here is picturing you in the tub, Madame. All soapy-bubbled and slick.

FANNY hits him and he laughs.

FANNY:

Shame on you! (*pushes MARTA's hands away*) I will do it!

MARTA:
You can't reach! Now lie still!

MARTA pulls FANNY's strings loose. FANNY moans in genuine agony.

I know. It just about killed me loosening my corset as the child grew. Like taking off my skeleton. But the muscles get stronger and it doesn't hurt as much. I can hold myself up now, though I'll never be twelve inches again.

FANNY:
No more Little Treasure.

MARTA smoothes the salve over FANNY's back ribs and is shocked.

MARTA:
Oh my God, you're all broken up on the side! Like you've been kicked by a horse!

WILLIAM:
(*sits up*) What?

MARTA:
What happened?!

FANNY:
(*pause*) Mining accident.

MARTA:
I don't know how you can breathe, Fanny!

FANNY:
Do not fuss.

WILLIAM:
Is there anything I can do?

FANNY:
Do not fuss! Louis is gone. I will not speak bad of the dead. (*beat*) That is feeling good on my skin, Marta. Merci. Warm

me right up. If you do not mind, I will lie here like this for
the while.

MARTA:
Sure.

MARTA covers FANNY up again, tucks her in like a girl.

FANNY:
(*sounding vulnerable*) What if the wolves come and I am all
undone?

MACKEY:
Don't worry. (*pulls out her rifle*) I have your La Longue Carabine.

FANNY recites her lines from Mohican.

FANNY:
Mighty Mohican. "I could sleep in peace, with such a fearless
and generous-looking youth for my sentinel … "

*Lights dim as they snuggle in to sleep. Lights up, everyone stirs
awake. MARTA pulls FANNY's corset tight with a foot in the
middle of her back. WILLIAM wraps a stunted finger with a scrap
ripped from MARTA's petticoat. MACKEY enters with news.*

MACKEY:
Well, we have bad news.

WILLIAM:
What?

MACKEY:
The snowfall's been too heavy to go much further, the
sleigh's in another foot deep overnight. The team will dig
the horses as far as Cottonwood and that's it.

WILLIAM:
How far away are we from Barkerville?

MACKEY:
About thirty-five miles.

FANNY:

We are so close! Tomorrow is Christmas Eve! We cannot give up!

MACKEY:

I snowshoed this morning over to Ryder's, he said he's willing to lend us one of his curiosities.

We hear the sound of a camel in the background. Everyone looks alarmed.

WILLIAM:

(*rushing over*) What on earth was that?!

MACKEY:

A camel.

FANNY:

In the Cariboo?!

MARTA laughs incredulously.

MARTA:

What is it doing here?

MACKEY:

They were brought in as pack animals for the gold rush, but they stink to high heaven and scare the horses so nobody uses them anymore. He might just suit our purposes though. His legs are tall enough to get through the snow. He'll be able to carry the two ladies plus our bags. William and I can snowshoe.

WILLIAM:

What about the baby?

MACKEY:

Can you do it, Marta?

MARTA:

Ich bin eine starke deutsche Frau!

FANNY:

D'accord. But for me, I am never get on that smelly beast in two shakes! My petticoat will stink for years. You go ahead, William, go up there on that hump and protect Marta.

WILLIAM:
But—!

FANNY:
No arguing! A man is allowed to smell.

MACKEY:
(*speaking of the camel*) Watch the spit.

MARTA and WILLIAM get up on the camel while FANNY and MACKEY strap on snowshoes, and they start rehearsals on their journey.

FANNY:
Did your people use snowshoes, Mr. Mackey?

MACKEY:
No. Mohicans run so lightly, we don't even make tracks.

FANNY:
(*impressed*) Mon Dieu! Mr. Mackey, I do not know why you are not more bold about your heritage. It's not like you're a heathen foreigner slanty. If I was Mohican I would shout it from the top of the hill!

MACKEY:
(*gives a mighty Native grunt*) Huh!

FANNY:
(*admiringly*) An Indian can say so much with a grunt. (*new idea*) You know, we should bill you in the program as a real live Mohican playing the Mohican. The audience will love you. Put you in traditional head-dress. We could go on tour! Many people would pay a lot of money to see a real to life savage, especially in Europe.

MACKEY:
No.

FANNY:
Why not?

MACKEY:
Why don't you just stuff me and stick me in the museum?
You will bill me as a Canadian, that's all. I want to be an
actor, not a spectacle.

FANNY:
People will guess anyway that you are Mohican because you
look Oriental, no offense. The Original People walk from
China to here, across the land when it was joined. But only
the bravest come this far, the strong, to make a new savage
and noble nation.

MACKEY:
(*amused*) I guess that would technically make me Chinese.

FANNY:
(*confounded grunt*) Huh.

WILLIAM:
What do we need to rehearse next? I feel confident with
Christmas Carol, Lord knows we have all heard it a million
times.

FANNY:
Mr. Mackey, do you want to air your Hamlet soliloquies?

WILLIAM:
Ah, the tortured Dane ...

MACKEY:
(*discouraged*) I originally thought I wanted to play Hamlet
because I remember a sword fight, but now ... I just don't
understand.

FANNY:
What is wrong?

MACKEY:
He doesn't do anything. He just complains a lot and then
he dies.

WILLIAM bends over as though he has been stabbed,
dramatically appalled by this summation of Hamlet.

WILLIAM:
Ah! He is a tortured soul! What is there not to understand?!

MACKEY:
Well, he goes on and on about "quintessence of dust" and
poor Yorick and "To be or not to be." He's not a hero, he's a
depressing self-destructive little whelp!

WILLIAM:
He has good cause! "To be or not to be, that is the question."
If he breaks his holy vows he is damned ... and yet if he
carries out his bloody office he is damned. Either way he feels
the guilt of failure and he's oh so excruciatingly alone in this
world. Honestly, good God, with friends like Rosencrantz and
Guildenstern, he has no ballast at all save the ineffectual
Horatio. And examine the women in his life! One is a mad
little angel (*indicating MARTA*) and the other ... (*swinging his
arm towards FANNY*) is a wretched temptress queen who
makes *me* ride the camel like a half-whipped calf!

WILLIAM rips off FANNY's snowshoes and puts them on
himself, while articulating wildly, flailing his limbs.

Neither of them can he please, neither of them can he touch,
neither of them can he cause anything but disappointment.
And he loves them both desperately! "No more, and by a
sleep to say we end / The heart-ache, and the thousand
natural shocks / That flesh is heir to; 'tis a consummation /
Devoutly to be wished to die to sleep! / To sleep perchance
to dream, ay there's the rub ... " Now get *on* that camel!

WILLIAM throws away his flask too after taking the final
vicious swig, using his blighted frozen finger to make his point.

And he cannot just slip into a drunken oblivion and drown
in a puddle of whiskey either, his conscience pricks and he
fears the fate of his soul ... "For in that sleep of death what
dreams may come / When we have shuffled off this mortal

coil / Must give us pause—there's the respect / That makes calamity of so long life: / For who would bear the whips and scorns of time, / Th' oppressor's wrong, the proud man's contumely, / The pangs of disprized love ... " the wagon's delay, the twenty-foot snow drifts and the frost bite ... "but that the dread of something after death, / The undiscovered country, from whose bourn / No traveler returns, puzzles the will, / And makes us rather bear those ills we have, / Than fly to others that we know not of? / Thus conscience does make cowards of us all ... "

They are all a little dumbfounded.

MACKEY:
Thank you, Mr. Teller. That clarifies the text.

Lights change. They dismount the camel, unpack their bags and collect themselves. FANNY trades her big boots for her high heels again and makes herself presentable.

MACKEY:
It was seven o'clock on Christmas Eve
When finally we arrived.
Bill got a frost bit pinkie
But every other bit of us survived.

Outside Barkerville we stopped on the road
And Fanny walked the last mile.
She laced up her corset and high-heeled boots
And teetered to town in style.

FANNY:
I'm off to see Mr. Bowron, the theatre manager, to tell him we're ready to do the show. This man is the beginning of my future!

MARTA:
I don't feel ready to present anything. We'll get booed off the stage!

WILLIAM:

Not at all, Marta. Look around you. They're all miners, nothing but grunting Philistines.

MACKEY:

It's true, they're so culturally deprived if you pass wind they'll applaud.

Aside to the audience.

Friends, no offense about your way of life.
It's more than a man deserves.
I only made fun to assuage my wife.
Try to pacify her nerves.

We warmed our toes in the Kelly Hotel
With no moment left to spoil.
Fanny went out to ring the show time bell
At the Theatre Royal.

MACKEY, WILLIAM and MARTA clear off, leaving FANNY to enter the theatre alone, tentatively.

FANNY:

Allo? Mr. Bowron? Allo? It's Madame Fanny Dubeau a.k.a. George Blake of the Pageant Players. Are you here?

BOWRON speaks from the back of the audience balcony, a disembodied voice, almost as though he were Deity. This startles FANNY.

BOWRON:

Yes, Madame. Up here. What brave magi you are, bringing us Christmas by camel! I told the town that if you arrived in time to perform the Christmas Eve pageant I would ring the bell at seven, which it is now, and have the show at eight. Is that enough time?

FANNY:

Ah, oui! We are professionals, Monsieur!

BOWRON:

That is funny, being from London, I expected you to have an English accent ...

FANNY:

I ... I ... (*suddenly tries to do an accent, sounds dreadful*) Right. Cheerio, tea time and all that, ta ta ...

BOWRON:

Pardon?

FANNY:

I'm speaking in English!

BOWRON:

(*searching*) Oh, is it ... Northern England?

FANNY:

South. So far south it is on the border of France.

BOWRON:

Ah. Well. Again, a delight to have you!

FANNY:

Good! So, what would you like to see first? We can do *Hamlet*, or *The Last of the Mohicans*, or *A Christmas Carol*. If you like comedy, I also have a little bit risqué burlesque called Fanny's Frolics ...

BOWRON:

Oh, wonderful! Maybe later on in the season. But tonight, we have our hearts set on seeing your famous Christmas play.

FANNY:

(*improvising wildly*) Right. Well we have several ... which story did you prefer?

BOWRON:

The Christmas story.

FANNY:

(*digging for clues*) We ... uh ... which author in particular took your fancy?

BOWRON:
Oh. Well. I suppose Luke.

FANNY:
Luke who?

BOWRON:
St. Luke.

FANNY:
(*sudden realization*) Oh! *The* Christmas story. We do the actual Jesus in the manger do we?

BOWRON:
Don't you?

FANNY:
(*back-pedalling*) Oui! We're famous for that. It is a little ... non-traditional ...

BOWRON:
But accurate. We do not want to offend anyone.

FANNY:
Ah oui. We have a reverend to keep us on book. Holy Book.

BOWRON:
Oh yes, and I do have one artistic stipulation. I ask that you do not treat the birth of Christ too realistically. We do not want to offend the ladies.

FANNY:
Right.

MACKEY:
And Harod's slaughter of the babes needs to be tasteful.

FANNY:
But of course.

MACKEY:
Good then, I'll leave you to the stage while I gather up an audience. Ta.

BOWRON is gone.

FANNY:

Ta. I promise, no blood! No screaming! That is why we do *Hamlet* and not *Macbeth.* (*suddenly realizes what she has said*) Oh no! Bordel! What have I done?!

She starts hopping around on one foot. MARTA enters and notices FANNY.

MARTA:

What is wrong with your foot?

FANNY:

It is in my mouth! I said the Scottish play! In the theatre! It is bad luck!

MARTA:

(*thick*) What, you mean *Macbeth?*

FANNY:

(*screams*) Do not say that! I cannot remember how to reverse the curse, hop on one foot. Oui! Now!

MARTA:

Mon Dieu!

FANNY:

Plug your nose and flap the arms and run around the building once. No, ten times. Do it! Go, go go! Vite!

MARTA circles as best she can as WILLIAM enters.

WILLIAM:

Why is Marta running around the building?

FANNY with her nose plugged and flapping her arms.

FANNY:

Because she said the thane of Cawdor!

WILLIAM:

Macbeth? (*realizes*) Blast!

FANNY:
AHHH! Quick, hop!

*FANNY starts running circles opposite to MARTA then
WILLIAM starts his, when WILLIAM passes FANNY,
she asks him various questions.*

FANNY:
Do you remember the Christmas story, the one from the
Bible?

WILLIAM:
Yes, of course.

Another lap.

FANNY:
Do you know it word by the word?

WILLIAM:
It has been such a long time ...

FANNY:
Keep going, Marta, we can't pay for the bad luck!

Another lap.

Do you remember un petit of the plot and the characters?

WILLIAM:
Yes.

FANNY:
Good. Then it is not so impossible!

WILLIAM:
What is?

MARTA stops, doubled over. The others still run laps.

MARTA:
Fanny, I can't keep running. We need to find a midwife!

FANNY:
What?!

MARTA:

I'm getting contractions!

FANNY:

Can't you hold it?

MARTA:

This is one entrance I can't predict!

FANNY:

You MUST! We need the immaculate conception! Marta, do your best to get through all the performance. It is only an hour away.

MARTA:

I'll try, just don't tell Joe, it will make him too nervous.

WILLIAM pulls in from his last lap, puffing for air. MACKEY arrives, everyone gathers around FANNY.

MACKEY:

I've finished unloading. What play do they want to see?

FANNY:

They want the Christmas Story: Jesus, Mary and Joseph.

MACKEY:

But we don't do that one!

FANNY:

We do now! Dieu nous aident!

WILLIAM:

The holy nativity?!

FANNY:

Do not argue!*(frantically rattles it off)* William, you be the narrate, Marta play Mary and Joe will play Joseph. Fly by your pants like the pigs. Use the costume, prop, whatever line seem to fit. If we do not perform, they will know that we are not the Pageant Players and we will not get paid! I lose the theatre, we lose the season, there's no work, we stuck here and mon Dieu, maybe we end up in the jail even!

ALL:
What?!

WILLIAM:
They think *we* are the Pageant Players?

FANNY:
Oui! The letter, the money, the tickets, was suppose to be for them, but I pretend it was for us.

WILLIAM:
That's ... that's ... You lied to us!

FANNY:
Yes I did. So hang me by my lips! (*pause*) What are you all looking at me like pie eyes? Hm? What I did, I did. Too late now.

WILLIAM:
I can't lie ...

FANNY:
Tell you this, we do the show, we prove our self, then later, I tell them the truth when they love us.

MARTA:
We need the money.

MACKEY:
(*anxiously admits*) There's no other work for the winter up here, we'll be stuck if we don't do the show ...

FANNY:
Listen to the Mohican, he's wise!

WILLIAM:
Fanny, never mind condoning, I can't execute this!

FANNY:
Why not?

WILLIAM:
I'm not fit to speak the Gospel.

FANNY:
But you are the only one who knows the scriptures!

MACKEY:
I hardly know the story …

MARTA:
Why can't you play Mary, Fanny?

FANNY:
Because, you are the one with child, c'est parfait.

MARTA:
I'm not playing the Mother of God!

FANNY:
Regardez, we are short on saints here … I am going to have to cast the sinners! Do you really want to deprive the audience? They're all wait for the Christmas.

MACKEY:
Marta, you look flushed. How are you feeling?

MARTA:
(*strained*) Fine. Let's do the show.

WILLIAM:
Fanny, you promise to tell them the truth after the performance?

FANNY:
Oui.

MACKEY:
I want to play Hamlet.

FANNY:
Everyone?

MACKEY / MARTA / WILLIAM:
Agreed.

FANNY:
Bon.

WILLIAM:
Let the babe be born.

*A green curtain suddenly drops in behind them all. Lights
change. Applause is heard, then dies out. Behind the curtain,
the cast whispers frantically.*

WILLIAM:
We just got the signal from Mr. Bowron, everyone's in the
house.

MACKEY:
But I haven't finished writing the prologue!

FANNY:
Never mind, get out there, Go! Go! GO! Break a leg.

MARTA:
I just broke water!

MACKEY:
(*shocked*) What?!

*MACKEY is obviously shoved through the curtains, and faces
the audience in shock, suddenly hiding his prologue notes, trying
to remember it from heart. He starts his speech nervous but
grows in confidence.*

MACKEY:
Our first debut tonight in scenic art—
With falt'ring accents, and with beating heart,
We come before you, nerves and feelings strain,
'Til step by step your confidence we gain.
And if your plaudits strike our anxious ear,
Care trembling flee, pursued by tim'rous fear.
A motley crew we dare to grace your stage.
The smell of camel slightly off the page.
We bring a tender irony to yarn
We hope befits a saviour born in barn.
We call you friends, the friends we know you now,
Pleased when you smile, and gratified, we bow.

He hurries behind the curtain and WILLIAM enters with a huge stockinged step, poised rigidly as Scrooge. There is a silence of the terrified about him. Eventually he is joined by the other actors who enter in various costumes, equally dazed with anxious fright.

WILLIAM:

(*his best Edmund Kean*) There was in the days of Herod a certain priest named ... (*trying to remember*) Zephaniah Haggai Malachi ... ZECHARIAH! And his wife was of the daughters of Aaron: Elisabeth.

FANNY quickly enters dressed as Mrs. Cratchit and poses as Elisabeth with a dramatic gesture.

They had no child, because Elisabeth was barren.

FANNY does a dramatic gesture for barren.

And they both were now well stricken in years.

FANNY is immediately stricken with extreme age and exits with flourish.

There appeared unto him an angel of the Lord.

MARTA enters as the ghost of Marley with her head in the knocker of the door, shaking chains.

MARTA:

(*ghostly voice*) Scrooge ... Ebenezer Zechariah Scrooge ... !

WILLIAM:

Humbug.

MARTA:

You don't believe in me.

WILLIAM:

I don't. You may be an undigested bit of beef, a blot of mustard, a crumb of cheese ...

Bells ring and MARTA howls through a contraction.

How now! What do you want with me?

MARTA:
Much!

WILLIAM:
You're particular for a shade. Can you sit down?

MARTA:
I can. *(lets out a very female groan)* Your wife will bear you a son.

WILLIAM:
(trying to keep the story going) And thou shalt call his name John the Baptist?

MARTA:
Yes! Or you will be haunted by three spirits.

WILLIAM:
The Trinity! Father, Son and Holy Ghost. And he will make ready a people prepared for the Lord.

MACKEY appears as Magua from The Last of the Mohicans, *and yells a huge war whoop, running on with FANNY, still as Elisabeth, dragged by the scalp. He proudly shouts.*

MACKEY:
Some of the people the Great Spirit made with skins brighter and redder than yonder sun, and these did fashion to his own mind. They were brave; they were just; they were happy!

FANNY notices his bare chest no longer has the blue turtle tattoo; she searches frantically around his body for it.

FANNY:
Where's your blue turtle tattoo?! You're not Mohican, you lied to me!

MACKEY answers her defiantly in Chinese.

MACKEY:
Kat boon loi chui koi gei nin!

He disappears. Everyone stands a little stunned by the non sequitur for a minute. MARTA hides another contraction and yowls as Marley.

MARTA:
Hear me! I am Gabriel, and I have been sent to tell you this good news. Elisabeth shall conceive!

FANNY:
(*suddenly back in character as Elisabeth*) But I'm an old woman!

WILLIAM puts his hand over FANNY's mouth.

WILLIAM:
And behold thou shalt be dumb, and not able to speak, until the day that these things shall be performed.

MACKEY runs on and stuffs something under FANNY's apron to make her suddenly round-bellied. She doesn't quite know what to say.

FANNY:
God bless us, everyone.

Everyone exits except for WILLIAM, who sighs with relief then braces for the next scene.

WILLIAM:
And the angel Gabriel was sent from God unto a city of Galilee, named Nazareth, to a virgin espoused to a man whose name was Joseph.

MARTA enters. She is dressed as Ophelia. MACKEY, in Hamlet's costume, enters as JOSEPH and is on his knee having just proposed. MARTA speaks to WILLIAM, talking of Joseph/Hamlet.

MARTA:
He hath given countenance to his speech, my lord, / With almost all the holy vows of heaven.

WILLIAM:

The angel came in unto her, and said …

FANNY enters dressed as Ghost of Christmas Past covered in fruit and vegetables. FANNY rattles off what she can remember of being a Catholic.

FANNY:

The Lord is with thee, blessed are thou among women and blessed is the fruit of thy womb Jesus. Holy Mary Mother of God pray for us sinners now at the hour of our death. Amen.

MARTA has another contraction that she tries to mask. She drops character, and breaks with pain and tears.

MARTA:

I can't do this … I can't … I'M GOING TO HAVE A BABY!

FANNY:

(sincere) Yes you are, and you are to give him the name … Jesus. Fear not, Marta—Mary.

WILLIAM:

Thou hast found favour with God.

FANNY tenderly wipes the strands of hair from MARTA's face. This becomes a real moment between the two. WILLIAM prompts MARTA's next line, and FANNY scuttles off to return as Elisabeth / Mrs. Cratchit.

WILLIAM:

You say, "how will this be seeing I know not a man?"

MARTA:

(whispers back) I can't say that.

WILLIAM:

(whispers the prompt again) How will this be …

MARTA:

(performing) How will this be seeing I know not a man?

WILLIAM:

The Holy Ghost shall come upon thee, and the power of the Highest shall overshadow thee, for with God nothing shall be impossible.

MARTA:

I will obey, my Lord.

FANNY as pregnant Elisabeth/Mrs. Cratchit, and stands beside MARTA.

WILLIAM:

When Elisabeth heard the salutation of Mary, the baby leaped in her womb, and Elisabeth was filled with the Holy Ghost.

MACKEY pulls out a tiny concertina and wheezes an intro to "Buffalo Gals," and FANNY dances her burlesque dance as pregnant Elisabeth around MARTA. Everyone sings.

EVERYONE:

BLESSED ARE YOU OH MOTHER OF GOD MOTHER OF GOD MOTHER OF GOD, BLESSED ARE YOU OH MOTHER OF GOD AND BLESSED BE THE CHILD IN YOUR WOMB! WHEW!

FANNY does the ringing of the bell with WILLIAM and baby John the Baptist flies out from underneath her skirts. MACKEY catches the "child" and hands it back to WILLIAM/Zechariah/ Scrooge, who is elated with the baby.

WILLIAM:

And Zechariah spoke: I don't know what to do! I am as light as a feather, I am as happy as an angel, I am as merry as a school-boy. I am as giddy as a drunken man. This is John the Baptist, who will announce the coming of the Christ child! He will live in the Past, the Present and the Future! A happy New Year to all the world!

Everyone exits except for WILLIAM, who sobers.

Now the birth of Christ was on this wise. When as his mother Mary was espoused to Joseph, before they came together, she was found with child of the Holy Ghost.

MARTA waddles on as Mary/Ophelia. MACKEY enters as Hamlet/Joseph and feigns to be shocked at her condition.

Joseph, being a just man, and not willing to make her a public example, was minded to put her away privily.

MARTA's contractions are regular now, but she masks them as best she can. It should be a struggle, but she does not scream. She gives him back his ring.

MARTA:
Joseph, I have remembrances of yours, / That I have longed long to re-deliver. I pray you now receive them.

MACKEY:
No, not I. I never gave you aught.

MARTA:
My honoured Lord, you know right well you did, and with them words of so sweet breath composed as made the things more rich. Their perfume lost, take these again.

She gives him back the ring.

MACKEY:
I did love you once.

MARTA:
Indeed, my lord, you made me believe so.

MACKEY:
Get thee to a piggery! Nunnery!

MARTA:
Oh heavenly powers, restore him!

MACKEY:
I say we will have no mo' marriage!

MARTA:

O, woe is me!

MARTA is carried off by FANNY/Cora Monroe/angel. FANNY
stands close by her exit, and masks her cries by singing Halleluiah
really loudly and indiscriminately. She flutters her "angel wings"
while hurriedly carrying back and forth a bucket of water and
costumes preparing for the birth. MACKEY starts to become
suspicious.

MACKEY:

Is she … is she … is she having the baby?!

WILLIAM continues, flustered, dressed as the Ghost of
Christmas Present.

WILLIAM:

But while he thought on these things, behold, an angel of
the Lord appeared unto him in a dream …

MACKEY as Hamlet/Joseph enters again and sees the ghost.
He keeps looking back towards where MARTA made her exit,
greatly distressed and distracted.

MACKEY:

Angels and ministers of grace defend us! King, Father, Royal
Dane. Is she having the BABY?!

WILLIAM:

(*ghostly voice*) Joseph, thou son of David …

MACKEY:

Speak, I am bound to hear!

WILLIAM:

Fear not to take unto thee Mary thy wife: for that which is
conceived in her is from the Holy Ghost.

MACKEY:

Oh, my prophetic soul!

WILLIAM:

They shall call his name Emmanuel, God with us.

MACKEY:

So be it!

MACKEY exits hurriedly to be with MARTA.

WILLIAM:

Joseph went unto Bethlehem, to be taxed with Mary, being great with child. And there were shepherds abiding in the field, keeping watch over their flocks by night.

MACKEY is obviously shoved out the exit with Indian head-dress on.

MACKEY:

(gives Mohican grunt) Huh!

WILLIAM:

And lo, the angel of the Lord came upon them ...

FANNY enters as the angel/Cora.

And they were sore afraid.

FANNY:

(as Cora) What are you looking at, sir?

MACKEY:

(As Uncas) I'm looking at you, miss.

MARTA cries out, runs backstage. FANNY tries to continue.

FANNY:

For unto you is born this day a Saviour, ye shall find the babe wrapped in swaddling clothes, lying in a ... lying ... *(breaks character and shouts)* Mon Dieu, we're not the Pageant Players! I lied! We're just a bunch of actors too poor to pay the bank and wolves were at our throats and we needed the money and it's all my fault so put me in the jail and swallow the key but, mais s'il vous plaît, she's giving birth to a real baby back there, IS THERE A DOCTOR IN THE HOUSE???

MARTA lets out her final push and we hear a baby cry. Silence. Confusion is starting to be heard in the audience, MACKEY shouts, triumphant, running onstage in amazement, holding a naked, bloody, squealing newborn.

MACKEY:

It's a boy!

WILLIAM:

(*elated, cries out*) Glory to God in the highest, and on Earth peace, good will toward men!

MARTA enters, staggering, absolutely covered in blood from the waist down, holding her fists triumphantly over her head, shouting in her happy hysteria.

MARTA:

Ich bin eine starke deutsche Frau!

MACKEY sees MARTA and plunks the baby in FANNY's arms to carry MARTA off stage again. FANNY holds out the baby as though it were a hot potato, looking terrified at it.

FANNY:

Don't give it to me! I don't know what to do with it! I—I ... (*softens suddenly as she looks into the eyes of the child, tenderly, broken*) look at you!

She sobs and hands the babe over to WILLIAM and runs out. WILLIAM is so shocked, he continues the story, holding the baby out at arm's length, not sure what else to do. As he speaks, however, he becomes impassioned, realizing the impact of his words as he holds the newborn.

WILLIAM:

The true light which lighteth every man that cometh into the world. He was in the world, and the world knew him not. He came unto his own, and his own received him not. But as many as received him, to them gave he power to become the children of God, which were born not of blood, nor of the will of the flesh, nor of the will of man, but of God.

Applause. He sweeps his hand dramatically, black out. In the darkness we hear FANNY struggling to escape outside in the storm. The wind is blowing snow into her face, she stumbles and falls. MACKEY narrates.

MACKEY:

A standing ovation ended our show
Only men came out to bow.
Marta was recovering, as you know
And Fanny escaped somehow.

FANNY falls in the snow, shivering. WILLIAM yells after her. She struggles to run away from him, but he catches up.

WILLIAM:

Fanny ... Fanny!

FANNY:

Blame me for everything, but let me go!

WILLIAM:

Come back!

FANNY:

(*shouts*) Leave me alone!

He has caught up with her and holds her by the arm as she struggles to get away, very upset.

WILLIAM:

There is nothing out here but snow! You are going to freeze to death!

FANNY:

(*struggles*) I don't care. My heart is so full of the lies, William, I don't know if I stand up or if I sit down anymore ...

WILLIAM:

(*firm*) There is nowhere to run.

FANNY:

I was at the rock bottom of my rope when that letter came ... let the wolves rip my bones ... (*cries and sinks in his arms*) Everything is gone ... the show was terrible, they will not pay, I can never get back to San Diego, my saloon is lost to the bank … and all I have done to you and Marta and the other one.

WILLIAM:
They loved the show, Fanny.

FANNY:
What?

WILLIAM:
Thank God for artistic deprivation. You've got to come back with me.

FANNY:
To what?

WILLIAM:
To us. To the theatre, to tell the truth. Come on. You can do it. It's an excellent time of year to ask for grace.

FANNY:
Mon petit chou. I thought you gave up preaching?

WILLIAM:
I did. That was an actor's dénouement monologue.

This makes her laugh a little and WILLIAM pulls her up firmly and kisses her. She almost faints in astonishment, but is rather pleased. He carries her through the snow. A spotlight comes up on MACKEY, half out of costume, in the theatre, cradling his son. MARTA is beside him, sitting on a costume chest, bloody dress showing under a gauzy wrap of the Ghost of Christmas Present. MACKEY speaks to the audience.

MACKEY:
It's a silent night in the Cariboo
As black and cold as my cup.
I've a Yuletide tale to travel with you
Down the Fraser and back up.

You won't find red ribbon or mistletoe
In my wooly Christmas yarn.

But a baby birthed just as oddly so
As a King born in a barn.

So grab your bearskins and your boots, be bold
Cuddle up now don't be shy.
We've got many miles before we hit gold
If we don't come close we'll die.

> *MACKEY sits on the floor beside MARTA. She rocks the baby and sings gently and simply in German, while MACKEY listens contentedly.*

MARTA:
Stille Nacht, heilige Nacht
Alles schlaft, einsam wacht.
Nur das traite hoch heilige Paar
Holder knabe im ockigen Haar.
Schlaf in himmlischer Ruh
Schlaf in himmlischer Ruh.

> *Lights fade as snow flutters.*

THE END.

TRANSLATIONS

FRENCH

PAGE 11

Où êtes vous? Si ils sont parties je les tuerais! / Where are you? If you have left I will kill you!

C'est Madame Dubeau ici ... Allo? / It is me, Madame Dubeau ... Hello?

Maudit! / Damn!

PAGE 12

Bordel! / Brothel hell!

Mon Dieu! / My God!

PAGE 14

zut alors ... / darn it! ...

... petit chou ... / ... my little darling ...

PAGE 15

Oui! / Yes!

PAGE 16

Pardon? Qu'est-ce que vous avez dit? / I'm sorry, what did you say?

Vous parlez français?! / You speak French?!

PAGE 17

Pardonnez-moi. / Pardon me.

Pas du tout ... / not at all ...

... c'est terrible ... / ... it's terrible ...

PAGE 18

Pathétique! / Pathetic!

PAGE 22

Merci! / Thank you!

PAGE 23
Où est ça? / Where on earth is that?

PAGE 25
Oui! Oui! Bonne idée, William! / Yes! Yes! Good idea, William!

PAGE 27
Ça va ... / No matter ...

PAGE 30
Voilà! / Tada!

Bon! / Good!

PAGE 31
Tu serais fantastique! / You will be fabulous!

PAGE 32
Ciel! / Heavens!

Qu'est-ce que j'ai fait? / What have I done?

PAGE 37
Je suis du Canada! / I am Canadian!

PAGE 45
Pourquoi? / Why?

PAGE 47
Ecoutez ... / Listen ...

PAGE 48
Soyez debout. / Stand up.

PAGE 49
... s'il vous plaît ... / ... please ...

PAGE 50
... pour moi. / ... for me.

... mes amis. / ... my friends.

PAGE 51
Taisez-vous! / Quiet!

PAGE 56
Bonjour! / Hello!

PAGE 61
Pardonnez-moi … / No offence …

PAGE 63
Exactement. / Exactly.

Je ne peux pas. / I can't.

Cette question … / The question …

PAGE 66
D'accord. / Fine.

PAGE 74
Vite! / Quick!

PAGE 75
… *un petit* … / … a little …

PAGE 77
Dieu nous aident! / God help us!

PAGE 78
… *c'est parfait.* / … it's perfect.

Regardez … / Look …

BROKEN CHINOOK

PAGE 37
Ab'ba, okoke tyee potlatch dolla, konaway siwash mokst dolla Boston illahie konaway week! / The foreman will pay all Indians two dollars and fifty cents American a week!

Mesika momook kunamokst okoke kawkawak man kopa tahtlum pe mokst dingding shut! / You will work beside the China man, twelve-hour shifts!

Mesika mamook sinamoxt sun week koshe spose okoke illahee hyas cole! / You will work seven days a week until the ground freezes!

GERMAN

PAGE 46
Fichtelgebirge, in der Nähe meines Heims in Deutschland, mit all den Kiefern … / Fichtelgebirge, near my home in Germany, with all the pines …

… wo sind Sie jetzt Mutter? / … where are you now, Mama?

Ich bin eine starke deutsche Frau! / I am a hearty German woman!

Ich bin froh, daß Du es magst. / I'm glad you like it.

PAGE 53
Vollständig. / Completely.

Narr. / Fool.

PAGE 91
Stille Nacht, heilige Nacht / Silent night, holy night

Alles schlaft, einsam wacht. / All is calm all is bright.

Nur das traite hoch heilige Paar / Round yon virgin mother and child

Holder knabe im ockigen Haar. / Holy infant so tender and mild.

Schlaf in himmlischer Ruh / Sleep in heavenly peace

Schlaf in himmlischer Ruh. / Sleep in heavenly peace.

CHINESE *

PAGE 37
你知不知道我是甚麼人?
我不是法國人,
我亦不是紅蕃,
我或者是唐人,
我一定是加拿大人。

Nai dei ng dei tui or hai ai sui? Or ng hai fa guo nin, or yiu ng hai gwei lo, or wat che hai hong nin, or yit ding hai ga na dai nin. / Don't you know who I am? I am not French, I am not Indian. I might be Chinese, and I am definitely Canadian!

PAGE 82
他們本來是原居民。

Kat boon loi chui koi gei nin! / They were the firstborn nation!

---

* Depending on the specific region in China from which they had originated, Chinese immigrants who came to the Cariboo during the gold rush spoke a variety of dialects. The phonetic transcription provided here is that of Taishanese (or Toisanese), which was one of the most commonly spoken and understood dialects within the Chinese communities across North America in the nineteenth and early twentieth centuries.